STEP-UP
GEOGRAPHY

Scotland

Alan Rodgers and Angella Streluk

Evans

Published by Evans Brothers Limited
2A Portman Mansions
Chiltern Street
London W1U 6NR

© Evans Brothers Limited 2006

Produced for Evans Brothers Limited by
White-Thomson Publishing Ltd,
Bridgewater Business Centre,
210 High Street,
Lewes, East Sussex BN7 2NH

Printed in China by New Era Printing Co. Ltd .

Project manager: Ruth Nason

Designer: Helen Nelson, Jet the Dog

Consultant: Grant Stewart, Faculty of Education,
University of Glasgow

British Library Cataloguing in Publication Data

Rodgers, Alan, 1958-

   Scotland. - (Step-up geography)

   1. Scotland - Geography - Juvenile literature

   I. Title. II. Streluk, Angella, 1961-

   914. 1'1

ISBN-10: 0 237 53097 X

13-digit ISBN (from I Jan 2007) 978 0 237 53079
6

Picture acknowledgements:

Camera Press: pages 14b (Ian Rutherford), 15b
(David Cheskin), 21t (Phil Wilkinson/TSPL); Corbis:
pages 1/16b (Vo Trung Dung/Corbis Sygma), 5
(Peter Turnley), 9 (Roger Antrobus), 13t (Jason
Hawkes), 14t (Wild Country), 15t (Michael Callan;
Frank Lane Picture Agency), 17b (Macduff Everton),
18 (Kevin Schafer), 26b (Wally McNamee); Rhona
Dick: pages 4bl, 25; Chris Fairclough: page 19b;
Doug Houghton Photography: cover (main) and
pages 4br, 10, 11b, 13b, 16t, 20, 21b; Helen
Nelson: page 4bc; Alan Rodgers: page 19t; Still
Pictures: page 26t; Topfoto: pages 12, 17t, 22, 23t,
23b, 24t, 24b, 27.

The map on page 11 is reproduced courtesy of the
Southern Uplands Partnership. Other maps by
Helen Nelson.

Also available: *Step-up Geography: Scotland*

Further titles relating to Scotland in preparation:
Step-up History: Mary Queen of Scots
Step-up History: Famous Scots

914·1

Contents

Where and what is Scotland? 4

What is Scotland made of? 6

Weather and climate 8

The Southern Uplands 10

The Central Lowlands .12

The Grampians 14

The North-West Highlands and Skye 16

The islands 18

Urban and rural living .20

Making a living 22

Getting about 24

Looking after the environment 26

Glossary 28

For teachers and parents 30

Index 32

Where and what is Scotland?

This book is about the physical and human geography of Scotland.

Scotland is the most northerly part of the island of Great Britain. It forms about one third of the island's area.

Did you know?

Great Britain	The island made of Wales, England and Scotland
The British Isles	Great Britain, Ireland and the many smaller adjacent islands
The United Kingdom	England, Scotland, Wales and Northern Ireland

Scotland is in the Northern hemisphere.

Landscape

Scotland has a rugged coastline with many islands, inhabited and uninhabited. Much of the land is made up of hills and mountains. The areas around the coasts and in the Central Lowlands are mostly lower and more gently sloping.

▶ *The thistle is an emblem of Scotland. You might find it on some £1 coins.*

Government

For hundreds of years Scotland was a separate country. It had a long line of monarchs, starting with Kenneth I, who reigned from 843 to 858. In 1603 James VI of Scotland also became king of England.

In 1707 Scotland and England were joined by a law called the Act of Union. From then Scotland was governed from London until 1999, when the Scottish Parliament took control of most Scottish affairs. Some things, such as defence, are still controlled by the UK Parliament at Westminster (London).

Scotland has its own legal and educational systems. Its local government is organised into 32 unitary authorities, which manage such matters as education, refuse collection, recycling, housing and social services.

The flag of Scotland is also the flag of the patron saint of Scotland, Saint Andrew. Look for it in the flag of the United Kingdom.

The people of Scotland

Scotland's two main languages are English and Gaelic. People in different regions speak in slightly different ways, called dialects.

Although it is a mainly Christian country, Scotland is increasingly multicultural. One result is that Scottish food specialities, such as haggis, are now part of a wider choice, including Indian and Chinese food.

Key Facts

Area	about 80,000 sq km
Population	about 5 million
Head of State	Queen Elizabeth II
Capital	Edinburgh
Average life expectancy	78 years for females, 73 years for males

Look up the same data for England, Wales and Northern Ireland.

▼ *These Highland Games winners are wearing traditional Scottish costume.*

What is Scotland made of?

From this map you can see that mountains, rivers and lochs make up much of Scotland's landscape. The coastline of the Scottish mainland is more than 6,700 km long. Many of the islands are too small to show on this map.

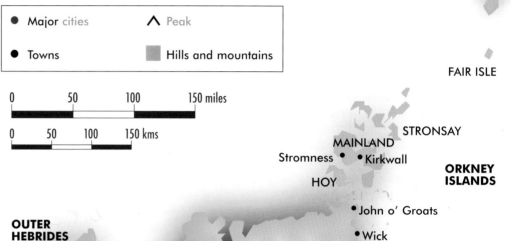

Legend	
● Major cities	∧ Peak
● Towns	▨ Hills and mountains

Scale: 0 — 50 — 100 — 150 miles
0 — 50 — 100 — 150 kms

Co-ordinates

Use an atlas map to find the co-ordinates of Scotland's

- longest river: River Tay, 188 km

- largest loch: Loch Lomond, 60 sq km

- longest loch: Loch Awe, more than 40.2 km

- highest point: Ben Nevis, 1344 m

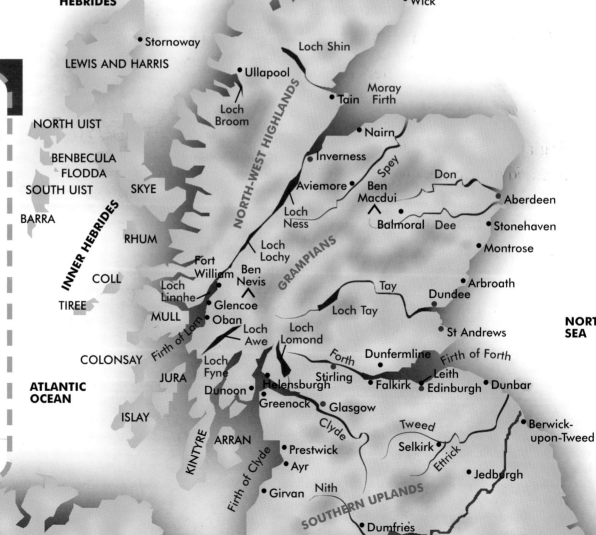

UNS

PAPA STOUR

SHETLAND ISLANDS

MAINLAND

Lerwick •

FAIR ISLE

STRONSAY

MAINLAND

Stromness • Kirkwall

ORKNEY ISLANDS

HOY

• John o' Groats

• Wick

OUTER HEBRIDES

• Stornoway

LEWIS AND HARRIS

Loch Shin

• Ullapool

Moray Firth

• Tain

Loch Broom

NORTH UIST

• Nairn

BENBECULA FLODDA

• Inverness

SOUTH UIST

SKYE

Spey

Don

BARRA

INNER HEBRIDES

Aviemore •

Ben Macdui

Aberdeen

Loch Ness

Balmoral   Dee

• Stonehaven

RHUM

Loch Lochy

GRAMPIANS

• Montrose

Fort William

Ben Nevis

Tay

• Arbroath

COLL

Loch Linnhe

Dundee

Loch Tay

TIREE

• Glencoe

• Oban

St Andrews

MULL

Loch Lorn

Loch Awe

Loch Lomond

NORTH SEA

COLONSAY

Firth of Lorn

Loch Fyne

Forth

Dunfermline

Firth of Forth

JURA

Stirling

Leith

Dunoon

Helensburgh

Falkirk

Edinburgh

• Dunbar

ATLANTIC OCEAN

Greenock

Glasgow

ISLAY

Clyde

Tweed

• Berwick-upon-Tweed

KINTYRE

ARRAN

Prestwick

Selkirk

Ettrick

Firth of Clyde

• Ayr

• Jedburgh

NORTH-WEST HIGHLANDS

• Girvan

Nith

SOUTHERN UPLANDS

Solway Firth

• Dumfries

Rock formation

The geology of Scotland tells an interesting story. The rocks that make up Scotland were formed up to 3 billion years ago, in different ways and in different places. Some came from lava from volcanoes, some from mud and sand sinking to the bottom of seas and some from hot deserts. Fossils can be found in many of the rocks.

Scotland drifts north

Millions of years ago the world looked very different. The lands that now make Scotland and England were separated by an ocean. They collided and joined 400 million years ago.

About 200 million years ago more continental drift caused all land areas to form Pangea, a huge supercontinent. Pangea later broke up to form the seven continents we have today. Scotland and England drifted slowly from south of the equator to their current position.

Landscape formation

Look on the map to see three fault lines in Scotland. These lines are where the different rocks that formed the land of Scotland

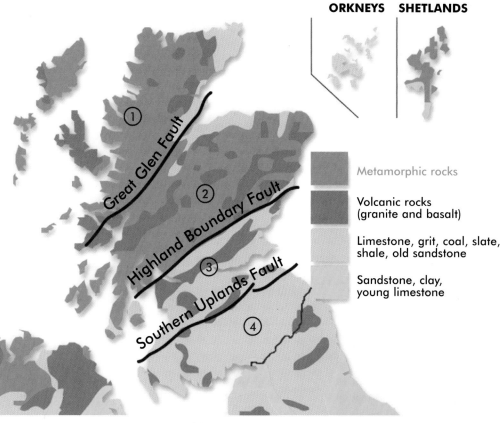

ORKNEYS SHETLANDS

Metamorphic rocks

Volcanic rocks
(granite and basalt)

Limestone, grit, coal, slate,
shale, old sandstone

Sandstone, clay,
young limestone

▲ The fault lines divide Scotland into four main regions: (1) the North-West Highlands, (2) the Grampians, (3) the Central Lowlands and (4) the Southern Uplands.

collided and joined together. The collisions caused mountains to form and lochs to appear. Use the key of the map to find the different rock types in each region.

Ice ages

During the many ice ages glaciers advanced and retreated. They gouged out valleys and left behind rocks when the ice melted. The last ice age was only 10,000 years ago.

Weather and climate

Scotland has a temperate climate. It experiences less extreme temperatures than Moscow, even though Scotland and Moscow are at the same latitude. This is due to the Gulf Stream, a warm ocean current driven by south-west winds from the Gulf of Mexico.

Scotland is generally cooler than the rest of the United Kingdom in the summer. However, the west of Scotland has similar January mean temperatures to south-east England.

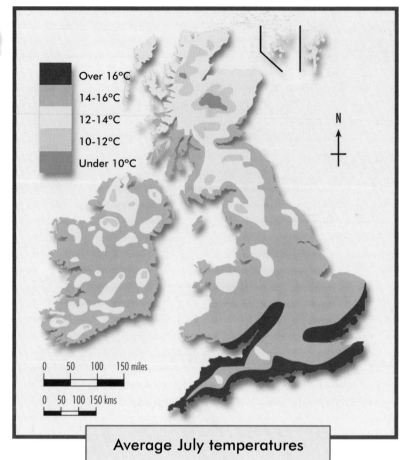

Over 16°C
14-16°C
12-14°C
10-12°C
Under 10°C

0   50   100   150 miles
0   50 100 150 kms

Average July temperatures

▲ *The higher the land, the cooler the mean*
◄ *temperatures. Which coast of Scotland stays milder than the rest of the country in winter?*

Varied weather

The weather varies across Scotland. In general, the west has more rain than the east. This is partly due to clouds forming as warm wet air from the Atlantic Ocean rises over the mountains.

The most common wind direction is south-westerly. Scotland has more strong winds and gales than any other part of the UK.

Average January temperatures

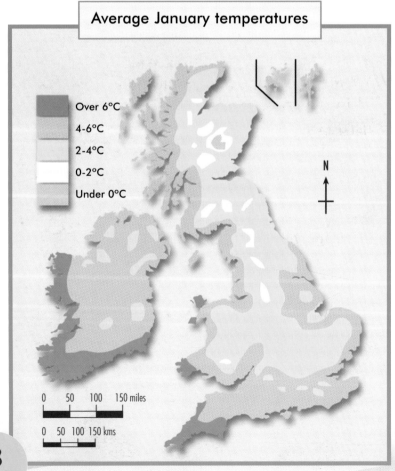

Over 6°C
4-6°C
2-4°C
0-2°C
Under 0°C

0   50   100   150 miles
0   50 100 150 kms

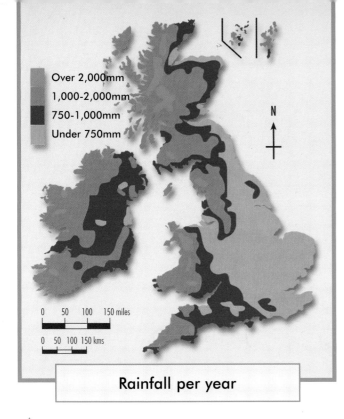

Rainfall per year

Legend:
- Over 2,000mm
- 1,000-2,000mm
- 750-1,000mm
- Under 750mm

0 50 100 150 miles
0 50 100 150 kms

▲ *Generally, Scotland has more rain than most of England. Why do you think the rainfall in northern Wales is similar to that in western Scotland?*

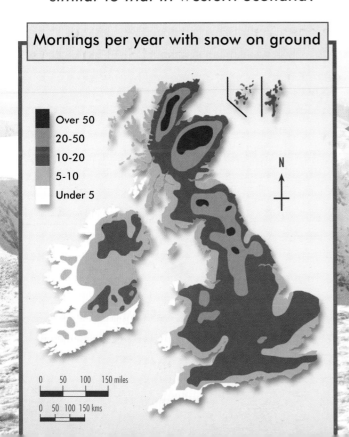

Mornings per year with snow on ground

Legend:
- Over 50
- 20-50
- 10-20
- 5-10
- Under 5

0 50 100 150 miles
0 50 100 150 kms

Climate change

There are some worrying predictions about how the climate will change if people do not change the way they affect the environment:

- Warmer winters could cause sea levels to rise. Coastal settlements could be flooded.

- Rainfall will increase in autumn and winter, but decrease in spring.

- Although there may be fewer gales, the ones that occur will be much more serious.

Weather data

Find weather data for different regions of Scotland from the Met Office web page: http://www.metoffice.gov.uk/climate/uk/location/scotland/index.html. How do you explain the differences at Lerwick, Aberdeen and Glasgow?

◀ *Where there are mountains, snow falls and stays for many days. The photograph shows the Cairngorm mountains.*

The Southern Uplands

The Southern Uplands region is named after the range of hills at its centre. The Southern Uplands Fault runs along its northern boundary.

The border with the north of England has not always been in the same place. It was fought over and changed many times in the past, especially between 1200 and 1500. Places like the town of Jedburgh were fortified, with castles and Scottish soldiers to protect them.

Coastal areas

Along the coasts, to the west and east, are strips of lower-lying land. Most towns, like Dumfries, are on this lower land. These towns have industrial areas, where various consumer goods are produced. Most of these are goods that can easily be transported by road.

The River Tweed

One of the least polluted rivers in the UK, the River Tweed has its source in the mountains of the Southern Uplands. Ettrick Water near Selkirk and other tributaries join the Tweed, turning it into a large river. When it reaches the lower land its valley forms part of a fertile farming area called the Merse. This land is used for sheep and cattle grazing and growing cereal crops, potatoes and animal feed.

◀ *People travel from all over the world to fish for salmon and trout in the beautiful surroundings of the River Tweed.*

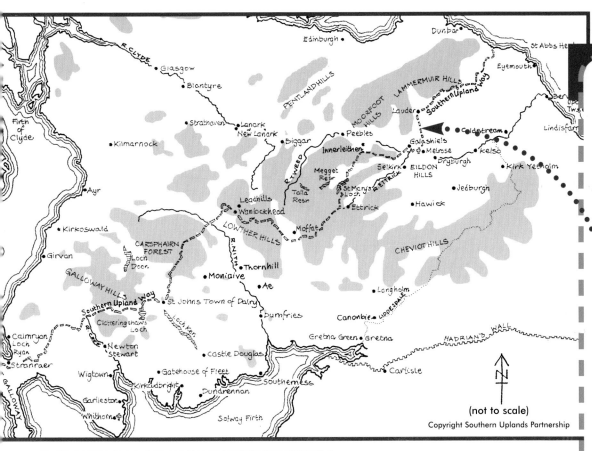
(not to scale)
Copyright Southern Uplands Partnership

The Southern Upland Way

People can enjoy the varied countryside by walking along the Southern Upland Way, a long-distance footpath linking the Irish Sea and the North Sea. It passes through the pine forests of the Galloway Forest Park, a protected environment which is managed to encourage wildlife and tourism.

Look at the route of the path on the map. Write a description of parts of a long walk along it. Mention the rise and fall of the route, crossing rivers and sightings of the seas.

The famous Scottish poet Robert Burns (1759-96) lived his last years in Dumfries. Tourists visit places linked with his life and work. This is the first verse of one of his poems, entitled 'Sweet Afton'.

Flow gently, sweet Afton! amang thy green braes,
Flow gently, I'll sing thee a song in thy praise;
My Mary's asleep by thy murmuring stream,
Flow gently, sweet Afton, disturb not her dream.

The Central Lowlands

The Central Lowlands lie between the Southern Uplands Fault and the Highland Boundary Fault.

The hills here are lower than in the rest of Scotland but the land is far from flat. Because the region is lower and flatter, it has more cities and built-up areas and more people live there than in the other regions.

Cities and rivers

The main cities are Glasgow, Dundee and Edinburgh. Each is near the mouth of a large river. Use the map on page 6 to match the cities to the Clyde, the Tay and the Forth. These rivers are deep enough for ocean-going ships to travel along and use the ports and harbours. Many manufacturing industries are based near the rivers. Ships used to be built on the Clyde.

Transport

The Central Lowlands contain more roads and railways than any other part of Scotland. The Forth Road and Rail Bridges are important in the transport system, shortening the distance from one side of the Firth of Forth to the other.

▲ The Forth Rail Bridge was the world's first major steel bridge. It has a special cantilever design. The Forth Road Bridge is a suspension bridge. When it was built in 1964, it had the longest span of any in Europe.

Compare distances

On a road map, find the distance from Edinburgh to Dunfermline (a) using and (b) without using the Forth Road Bridge. Check your distances with an Internet route finder, such as http://www.theaa.com/index.html. To find the distance without using the bridge, add 'via Kincardine' into the instructions.

Changing industry

Coal is found underground in the Central Lowlands. There used to be many deep coal mines, but now coal is only extracted by open cast mining. This has a large environmental impact because it is hard to put the land back to how it was before mining began.

Tourist attractions

Tourists are attracted to the interests of the big cities. They can travel there easily by rail and air. For walkers and others who enjoy the countryside there are many areas of natural beauty in Scotland. Scotland is where golf was first played, with St Andrews being home to the Royal and Ancient Golf Club. Golfers travel from around the world to play in Scotland.

▲ *Loch Lomond (above) and Loch Katrine supply water to central Scotland as well as being attractions for tourists.*

▼ *Edinburgh's castle, high on a volcanic rock, is one of the city's many attractions.*

13

The Grampians

This mountainous area lies between the Great Glen Fault and the Highland Boundary Fault. There are mountains in the middle, and lower land near the sea. Because of the rocky land there are fewer inhabitants per square kilometre and fewer transport links than in other parts of Scotland.

▲ There is almost always some snow on the peak of Ben Nevis.

Mountain range

The Grampians are a rugged and spectacular mountain range. They include Ben Nevis, the highest peak in the British Isles at 1,344 metres.

The second highest peak in Scotland, Ben Macdui, at 1,309 metres, is in the Cairngorm mountains, a high plateau of the Grampians. This is a cold, rocky desert environment where alpine flowers such as the starry campion grow. The Cairngorm funicular railway takes visitors to just below Cairngorm peak (1,245 m).

Using the mountains

In the winter the Grampians are popular with skiers. The resort at Aviemore provides accommodation and entertainment. In the summer the area is enjoyed for its spectacular views and mountain habitat. The Cairngorms National Park has been created to try to educate visitors to look after the fragile environment.

◀ Mountain-biking near Aviemore.

Forests and rivers

The mountains contain the sources of several large rivers including the Dee and the Don. The River Spey is the fastest-flowing river in Great Britain. This is caused by the steep descent through the mountains. Some rivers flow through forest areas, such as the Forest of Atholl. These forests provide a suitable habitat for unusual animals such as osprey, golden eagle, red squirrel and the Scottish wildcat.

▲ *This Scottish wildcat has caught a rabbit for its prey.*

Land use

The best farming land is on the eastern coast. Rainfall there is more even throughout the year, producing good grazing land. Breeds of cattle such as the Aberdeen Angus are world-famous for their quality of beef.

Inverness and Aberdeen, the main cities, are on the coast. Aberdeen has links with Scandinavia and the Baltic through its port. It also has transport links with oil platforms and drilling rigs in the North Sea.

▼ *Balmoral Castle is one of the most famous castles in Scotland with links to royalty and tourism. You can find out more at http://www.balmoralcastle.com/index.html. Other tourism centres include Montrose, Arbroath, Fort William, Oban, Dunoon and Nairn.*

Poster Poser

How does tourism help people who live in the area? What harm can people do in a fragile mountain environment? Use books and the Internet to find out more. Design a poster, *either* encouraging tourism in Aviemore in both summer and winter *or* outlining the bad effects of tourism.

The North-West Highlands and Skye

The North-West Highlands lie between the north and west coasts of the mainland and the Great Glen Fault. Loch Linnhe, Loch Lochy and Loch Ness are on this fault line.

The North-West Highlands mountain range contains several National Scenic Areas such as Glen Affric. Some of the last remaining parts of the Caledonian Forest, with its Scots pine, are found in the North-West Highlands.

The region has very few inhabitants because the mountainous terrain makes living here very difficult.

▲ In the far north-east of the mainland is John o' Groats, with its ferry to the Orkneys. Sponsored events often start or finish here.

Nessie's Scotland

Have you heard of Nessie, the monster said to live in Loch Ness (right)? Why would it choose to live in Scotland? Look for ideas in the pages of this book. Draw and label the things the monster loves.

Coasts

The west and north-west coasts are rugged and beautiful. Sea lochs, such as Loch Broom, cut into the land, often providing sheltered mooring for ports such as Ullapool. There are many sharp rocks along the coast because of erosion of the land by the prevailing wind and heavy rain. Ships are guided away from these rocks by lighthouses on the coast.

The Isle of Skye

The Skye Bridge, opened in 1995, joined the island of Skye to the mainland for the first time since the last ice age. This meant that the traditional ferry was no longer needed. Skye is still an island, but is easier to get to. At first there was a charge for using the bridge but now it is free. Find out about the controversy around the construction of this bridge. Skye contains a National Scenic Area called the Cuillin Hills, or the Cuillins.

Industry

Although there is little industry in the North-West Highlands and Skye, some products made here are world-famous. Caithness glass was first produced in Wick. Its colours remind you of the Scottish landscape: for instance, purple

▲ Erosion has led to many interesting rock formations, including cliffs, arches and stacks, such as the Duncansby Stacks.

for the heather. Whisky is also produced in this area, with a hint of a special smoky flavour in it. Fish farming has been developed in the sea lochs, making good use of the geography of the coasts.

▼ A famous whisky distillery is the Glenmorangie distillery, at Tain.

The islands

Besides the mainland there are 787 islands of Scotland. Most are uninhabited. People live on about 95 of them.

▶ *The island populations vary, as these examples show. In total, about 100,000 people live on the Scottish islands.*

Island	Population in 2001
Mainland Orkney	15,315
Hoy	392
Stronsay	343
Gairsay	3
Mainland Shetland	17,550
Unst	720
Papa Stour	25
Lewis and Harris	19,918
Flodda	11

◀ *The islands have some of the most interesting geology in the world. Find out which island Fingal's Cave is on.*

The Hebrides

The Hebrides are split into the Inner and Outer Hebrides. Lewis and Harris is the biggest island of all, having an area of 2,225 sq km. This island and those nearby produce Harris tweed, which is hand-woven in islanders' homes. Few large industries are located on the islands, but broadband Internet connections now make it possible to work from the region.

The Shetlands and The Orkneys

The Shetlands and Orkneys lie to the north-east of the mainland. The Shetlands are made up of 100 islands and islets, fewer than 20 of them inhabited. Look up some of their names in an atlas or online at http://www.multimap.com/. A main source of employment is the Sullom Voe Oil Terminal. Scatsta Airport is an important link to the oil rigs.

Fair Isle is 40 km south of the main group and is famous for a special style of knitting with an X and O pattern.

The Orkneys are a group of 90 islands, islets (holms) and rocky reefs. Only 21 of the islands are inhabited.

Island life

Island life is very different from mainland life. Transport to and from the mainland can be limited and people often have to manage with the resources on the island. They may need to do more than one job.

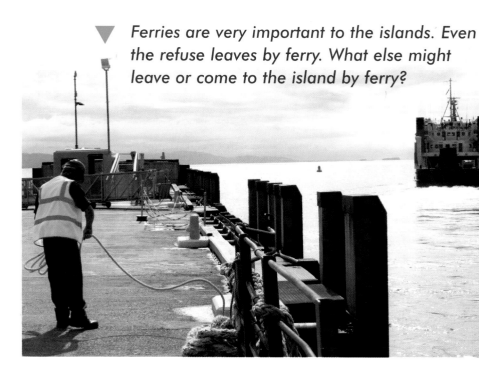

Ferries are very important to the islands. Even the refuse leaves by ferry. What else might leave or come to the island by ferry?

To earn a living I need to do more than one job. Not enough people live here to use my taxi a lot.

Key differences from living on the mainland are:

- There are fewer facilities, such as shops and hospitals.
- Water is often collected locally.
- Rugged land and poor soil make farming difficult.
- Transport to and on the island is limited.
- Lack of light pollution from street lights means that more stars are visible to the naked eye.

What other differences can you think of?

Similarities and differences

Some island children have to travel to the mainland to secondary school.

Island children – write about how you will feel when you have to go away to school.

Mainland children – list the things you have done and the places you have been during one week. Tick those you could still do if you lived on an island in Scotland.

Urban and rural living

Scotland's larger cities and towns are generally on the lower land, often near the coasts. Many are in the Central Lowlands. A large proportion of the total population – 82% – live in settlements of over 3,000 people. Although these settlements are home to most of the people, they do not cover much of the area of Scotland.

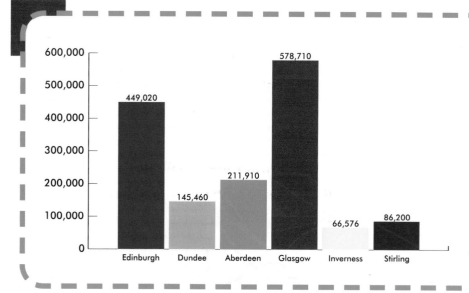

Locate the cities

The graph shows the populations of the main cities. Locate the cities on the map on page 6 and find which region they are in. How many are on lower, flatter land? What proportion is near the coast and what proportion inland? Is it more or less than half? Why do you think this is?

City life

The cities provide many facilities for the whole population. People usually need to go to the cities for specialist hospital care, university education and consumer goods. Art galleries and museums, such as the Museum of Childhood in Edinburgh, are mostly located

Inverness was made a city as part of the Millennium celebrations in 2000. It has grown considerably over the last few years.

in cities so that people can travel to them more easily. Cities are often the centres for business, industry and local government. Parks are sited in towns and cities as green areas of beauty.

Towns

Towns are important local centres for health care, secondary schools, colleges, retail centres and sports facilities. Look at some of the towns on the map on page 6. How many have a river running through them? What else do they have in common?

Life in rural areas

Some more remote, rural areas have smaller settlements. The main sources of employment here are farming, providing outdoor activities and fish farming. Castles and country parks and other sites of interest are often in these rural areas. In many cases, people living in rural settlements need to travel to towns and cities for access to facilities.

▲ *This building at Holyrood in Edinburgh was opened in the presence of Her Majesty the Queen on 9 October 2004. It houses the first Scottish Parliament since 1707.*

▶ *Some areas still have a type of farming called crofting. Many crofters do not own their property but rent it. They often have another job as well as farming their croft.*

Making a living

Scotland's economy

Exports from Scotland go mainly to France, Netherlands, the USA, Germany and Italy. About 70% of these are manufactured goods. In 2003 the USA was the country that imported the most from Scotland, with goods to the value of £2.5 billion. Food and drinks made up a large proportion of exports in 2003.

▶ *'Arbroath Smokies' are smoked haddocks prepared in the town of Arbroath. They have Protected Geographical Status. This means that only a smoked haddock from Arbroath can be called an 'Arbroath Smokie'.*

The work people do

The work people do is often divided into different categories. Read about the categories on these two pages. Find out what people in your local area do for a living and then graph your results using the four categories. Which type of work is most common? How does this compare to Scotland as a whole?

Service industries

Service industries do things for others rather than making an end product. The largest proportion of people in Scotland work in the service industries. Examples include working in shops and hotels.

Community services

Community services are also a form of service industry. They are the second largest type of employment in Scotland. Workers in community services include people employed in public administration, education and health and social services. Teachers and doctors are examples of workers in community services.

Community services are managed by the unitary authorities. The authorities cover different-sized areas: smaller where there is a high concentration of people, such as Inverclyde; and larger in rural or mountain regions (e.g. Aberdeenshire) where the population is spread out.

Manufacturing

When people manufacture things there is a product at the end of the process. Scotland's main products are office machinery, communications equipment, whisky and chemicals. These manufacturing industries

▼ *Call centres are a service industry. They became very common but now many are being relocated. They are moving to countries where workers receive less pay.*

provide work for many people. This is the third largest employment sector in Scotland.

Primary activity and utilities

Employment in the 'primary activity and utilities' category involves making use of the Earth's resources. 'Primary activity' includes farming, fishing, mining and quarry work. In Scotland it also includes working in forestry. 'Utilities' include the supply of electricity, gas and water services. These two sectors employ the smallest proportion of people in Scotland.

▲ *A gravel pit. Scotland has good-quality stone which is used as aggregate for road building. Some attempts to open huge quarries have not been allowed, in order to protect the countryside.*

Getting about

Think about the ways in which you have travelled from one place to another in the last month. Most methods of transport are used somewhere in Scotland. The routes they follow depend very much on the sort of land they cross. Mountains and firths mean that roads and railways often go the long way round to destinations.

Land travel

Roads are the most common transport network in Scotland. Their main advantage is that they lead even to the more remote settlements. There are several motorways but in many places roads have to weave their way through a difficult landscape. It would not be practical to build wide motorways there.

▲ *The M8 runs west to east across the Central Lowlands, passing through Glasgow.*

▶ *A narrow road winds through the gorge at Glencoe.*

A network of railways provides routes through Scotland and links with the rest of Great Britain and Europe. Tourists in Scotland often use the trains because of the beautiful scenery through which they travel.

Water transport

Ferries provide important links with the many islands in Scotland. Another water route is the Caledonian Canal, which links the east and west coasts. This canal is 96.5 kilometres long, but only 35.5 kilometres are man-made: the rest is formed by natural lochs. Look on a map to see which they are.

The Falkirk Wheel was built to reconnect the Forth and Clyde Canal to the Union Canal. It replaced eleven locks, which were demolished when the canals were no longer used. It cost £84.5 million to mend this link between the east and west coasts. It is hoped that the result will be that more visitors come to central Scotland.

Ports such as Aberdeen, Greenock and Leith help transport goods, imports and exports. These ports are also used as departure points for cruises to many destinations.

Taking to the air

Air travel is becoming more common in Scotland. People fly from international airports such as Glasgow, Edinburgh, Prestwick and Aberdeen to other places in Scotland and abroad. Other airports, such as Inverness, link some of the islands, the mainland, England, Wales and Northern Ireland.

▲ *The Falkirk Wheel rotates, allowing boats that have travelled along one canal to continue their journey along the next, although it is at such a different level.*

Travel symbols

Not only people but goods and animals need to be transported. There are many ways of getting about. On a map, airports are often shown with an aeroplane symbol. Look on a map and see how many symbols you can find that are linked to travel.

Looking after the environment

Scotland has large areas that are unspoilt and beautiful, but like everywhere in the world it has environmental problems.

Waste not want not

One concern is how to dispose of all the waste produced by homes and businesses. In Scotland more than 85% of this waste is sent directly to landfill sites. This compares to 78% in England. As more waste is produced, more landfill sites must be found. Another difficulty is that the buried rubbish produces the greenhouse gas methane.

Often things are thrown away to be replaced with new manufactured goods. More of the Earth's resources are used to produce the new goods. Also, many of the manufacturing processes are a source of gases that damage the environment.

▲ The plastic rings from a pack of drinks cans have killed this bird on a Scottish beach.

▼ What would you write and draw on a placard to persuade people to care for Scotland's environment?

Recycling

Think about your recycling and how this would help reduce waste. How much rubbish is collected from your home or classroom? What do you recycle? How many recycling centres are nearby? Why might recycling be more difficult in certain parts of Scotland?

Power and the environment

Everybody wants electricity, for commercial or domestic use, but producing it has an impact on the environment. Power stations that burn fossil fuels, such as coal, gas or oil, give out more greenhouse gases.

Scotland is lucky that it can produce power using two renewable resources – wind and water. Because of the landscape, many wind farms have been built. The mountainous landscape and heavy rainfall in certain areas mean that there is fast-flowing water. This can be used to turn the turbines to power the generators at hydro-electric power stations.

There is much discussion about how to supply more power. Nuclear power causes less immediate damage to the environment, but there are unsolved problems about disposing of nuclear waste.

▲ Wind power is clean and free, but turning it into electricity is costly and some people think that wind farms are a blot on the landscape.

Transport concerns

Many forms of transport, especially cars, cause air pollution. Sharing transport by using buses and trains instead of cars helps to reduce the impact on the environment. However this can be difficult in Scotland, because the population is spread thinly in remote locations.

Looking after Scotland

Whether you live in Scotland or visit it, remember that everything you do has an impact on the environment. Consider what you do and how you do it, so that there will still be a special Scotland for the future.

Glossary

aggregate   rocks used in the building process, often as a foundation for roads.

alpine   to do with high mountains such as the Alps.

Caledonian Forest   an ancient forest that once covered a vast area of the Scottish Highlands. Only small sections now survive.

canal   a man-made waterway, built to help carry goods and people but now often used for leisure activities.

cantilever   a beam that is fixed or weighted at one end. Such beams are sometimes used to hold up a very wide bridge.

cereal crops   grass plants grown for their seeds, which can be used for food. Wheat, barley and oats are examples.

Christian   a person who believes in and follows the teachings of Jesus Christ.

city   a settlement, often larger than a town. Some cities were granted this status for special reasons, such as having a cathedral.

continental drift   very slow movement of the continents, caused by movements within the Earth's crust.

co-ordinates   the numbers and letters which help to locate a place on a grid on a map.

crofting   farming a small plot of land in the Highlands and Islands.

erosion   the wearing away of rocks.

exports   things that are sold to other countries.

facilities   the things that people need to live comfortably, such as supplies of water and electricity, shops, transport etc.

fault line   a large crack in the rocks of the Earth's crust, caused by movement.

fertile   (of soil) good for growing plants, as it contains the correct nutrients.

firth   a strip of the sea stretching inland.

fossil fuels   fuels that come from fossilised plants and animals. E.g. oil, coal and gas.

fossils   remains or impressions of prehistoric plants or animals found in rocks.

funicular   mountain railway with two counter-balanced carriages linked by a cable.

gale   a strong wind with a speed of 45-90 kilometres per hour.

geology   the study of rocks.

glacier   a very slow-moving river of ice.

Great Glen Fault   the fault line stretching from Inverness to Fort William, and continuing under the sea towards Ireland.

greenhouse gas   a gas in the Earth's atmosphere which stops heat escaping into space. The effect is that the Earth heats up as if it were in a greenhouse.

habitat   the place where a plant or animal naturally lives, containing all that it needs and having the right sort of weather for its survival.

hemisphere   half of a sphere. An imaginary line called the equator divides the Earth into northern and southern hemispheres.

Highland Boundary Fault	a fault line stretching from Helensburgh to Stonehaven.
human geography	the study of the effect of humans on their surroundings.
landfill	a large hole in the ground used for the disposal of waste.
latitude	a measurement made using a series of imaginary lines around the Earth, to describe distance, north or south, from the equator. Similar lines running pole to pole are called lines of longitude.
lava	hot molten rock coming out of volcanoes and other cracks in the Earth's surface.
life expectancy	the age to which a person is expected to live.
lock	a step-like device which allows the water level of a canal to be raised or lowered where the land slopes. Vessels can go up or down using the locks.
mainland	the largest block of land in a country or group of islands.
manufacture	to make a product from raw materials, often using machinery.
mean temperature	the average temperature over a given period of time.
metamorphic rocks	rocks formed when existing rocks are changed by heat etc in the Earth's crust.
mouth	where a river flows into the sea or a lake.
National Scenic Area	an area given a special status by the organisation called Scottish Natural Heritage. National Scenic Areas are maintained with extra care so that their beauty can be appreciated.

open cast mining	removal of material from the ground by means of a large hole.
peak	the highest point on a mountain.
physical geography	the study of natural features in the environment.
plateau	a flat area of higher land.
prevailing wind	the most common wind direction.
quarry	a place where rock is taken from the ground, often a large industrial site.
reef	rock, coral or sand which is either just below or just above sea level.
renewable resource	a resource that can be renewed by nature, e.g. wind, trees.
rural	to do with the countryside.
sea loch	a loch that flows into the sea.
settlement	a place where people live in a community.
source	the start of a river or stream.
Southern Uplands Fault	a fault line stretching from Girvan to Dunbar.
temperate	rarely very hot or very cold.
terrain	type of land, e.g. a marshy terrain.
tributary	a stream or river flowing into another.
turbines	a series of blades which are turned by the power of the wind or a fluid, such as water.
unitary authority	a region of local government.
valley	a dip between two hills or mountains.

For teachers and parents

This book is designed to support a study of geography in the context of Scotland. It is intended that children will be able to use this book to explore elements of human and physical geography as they relate to Scotland. As expected in any locality study, all geographical skills can be used in a real context. The skills and concepts developed include the ability to:

- observe and question
- collect and record evidence
- use maps and plans
- use secondary sources
- undertake fieldwork
- appreciate the quality of an environment
- use ICT to access, analyse and present information
- communicate and explain issues
- understand different viewpoints.

SUGGESTED FURTHER ACTIVITIES

Pages 4-5 Where and what is Scotland?
When working on other contrasting localities children could use this page as a template. Read the page and make notes of key facts. Find out the same facts for the locality being studied.

The Government section may prompt discussion of the services managed by the children's local unitary authority. Which services and regulations are controlled locally? How do local people have a say in this? Who are the local representatives? This links well with Citizenship issues.

Also look at the locations and sizes of unitary authorities. Relate the areas to the population. Is the area consistently smaller for the more densely populated regions? Statistics can be found at the General Register Office for Scotland at http://www.gro-scotland.gov.uk/index.html in the Statistics Library.

Pages 6-7 What is Scotland made of?
Children could investigate how rocks are formed by visiting http://sln.fi.edu/fellows/payton/rocks/create/index.html.

They could find out about the geology of their local area. Explain how the data is presented on a map. This may also be a good opportunity to point out features on the map (e.g. the shape of the coast) which help pinpoint the home or school location. Locate the local area on the map and use the key to find out which sort of rock it is made of.

Which faults does it lie between? Has anybody seen evidence of the faults? Did they know about them before?

If possible, visit an area with rocks in their natural environment. Collect samples and use a hand lens to look closely at them. (Be careful not to damage the environment. Only go to places you have permission to visit.) Find out how the rock was formed. Compare it to other rock samples. Which is the hardest? Can any be scratched with a nail? Have minerals been extracted from the local area? What evidence remains?

Other sources of information may be local museums, reference books and the Internet. See some photographs of minerals found in Scotland on the Russell Society website at http://www.russellsoc.org/galsco.htm.

Pages 8-9 Weather and climate
Find your location on the weather maps. Read off the data using the keys. Choose a contrasting location in Scotland. Read off the data. How does it compare?

Use the Met Office website http://www.metoffice.gov.uk/climate/uk/location/scotland/index.html to look up data for the location nearest to you. Look at the dates of the weather data used to produce the graphs. This demonstrates the difference between weather and climate. Climate data always uses average figures over a long period of time.

Start collecting local weather data. This can easily be set up using either home-made equipment or inexpensive apparatus and kits. For information on setting up a weather station and how to collect good weather data see http://www.amingtonheath.staffs.sch.uk/intro.html.

Pages 10-11 The Southern Uplands
Work on rivers can be supported by this page. Read the paragraph on the River Tweed. Go through each sentence in detail, working out what jobs might be involved in each reference. For example, the first sentence shows that somebody must be checking the water quality. Make a list of people who make a living from the River Tweed. Add any more you can think of. An Internet search might bring up some more ideas, just by reading the search results. Remember to put UK in your search or you may be looking at the River Tweed in Australia! Which part of the river provides most employment?

The River Tweed flows through many different types of land. It might be good to revise what land use is and how it is reflected on large-scale maps. Look at a key on an Ordnance Survey map or use an interactive whiteboard and a website such as http://www.centremaps.co.uk/landranger-map-land-symbols.htm. Revise the different shadings and symbols. Then follow the River Tweed from its source to the sea at http://www.waterscape.com/River_Tweed/map/wid172;mine399240;maxe313401;minn635200;maxn653440. Zoom in and make a note of any evidence of land use around the river. Does it change as it flows through higher or lower land?

Pages 12-13 The Central Lowlands

The text implies that this area is the hub of Scotland and is central to transport systems. The capital city is also in this area, containing the seat of government. However, it might be interesting to find out if there is anybody who has no connections with this region whatsoever. Is there anybody who has never been to this area and has no relatives living there?

Use the pages in this book and the BBC Landscapes website to investigate the Central Lowlands. Use art skills to create a picture to submit to the Central Lowlands Gallery. Decide on a topic that portrays the Central Lowlands well. See the BBC Lowlands chapter at http://www.bbc.co.uk/scotland/education/sysm/landscapes/central_lowlands/flash/english_embed_audio.shtml.

Pages 14-15 The Grampians

Use the Mountains sections to set the scene for a study of other mountain ranges. Make a list of headings from the information on this page. Add information from the children's own experiences of the area. They might also ask friends and relatives, as part of a survey.

Use the same headings to search for data on other mountains or mountain ranges. Make a database of mountains or mountain ranges – use data on the Grampians or Ben Nevis to start it off. Excellent data can be found at http://en.wikipedia.org/wiki/List_of_mountains. Enter the data into a database or spreadsheet. Use the sort function to help analyse the data. Devise a set of questions to answer.

Pages 16-17 The North-West Highlands and Skye

This page could be used to help develop work on coasts. The description of the rugged coast caused by erosion may be difficult to imagine. A walk round the school grounds or local area could soon produce examples that are more easily understood. Look for evidence of soil washed away around rainwater downpipes, grass and soil worn away by feet, and wear caused by rubbing or banging.

Build a model coast from wet sand. Use a container of water to erode it. Try a trickle, then a deluge. Use a squeezy bottle to attack the cliffs of the model. A video of a coast with raging waves and wind battering the rocks would bring home the forces of nature. A field trip to see a rocky coastal area, with due regard for safety procedures, would be an excellent conclusion to this work.

Pages 18-19 The islands

Use the BBC Landscapes chapter on Islands to revise the island groups. Make notes ready for other work on islands. Are there any distinguishing features of Scottish islands? See the BBC site at http://www.bbc.co.uk/scotland/education/sysm/landscapes/highlands_islands/flash/index.shtml.

To fully realise the impact of living on an island it might be good to make a model of one. Use papier mâché, clay or plaster modelling strips to construct the model.
- Try to include physical features from other geography work.
- Revise features of coasts and include a variety of these. Will these remain the same over the years?
- What transport communications should be included?

- Where should the settlements be located?
- Look at the sea all round the island. What difference does this make to life?

Pages 20-21 Urban and rural living

Reading this page might stimulate a debate about preferences for rural or urban living. Is one always better than the other? Are there good and bad points in both? Think of Town Mouse and Country Mouse (a digital version can be found at http://www.umass.edu/aesop/fables.php). The children could write a letter – either town person to country person or vice versa – saying why they should move. They might want to be fair and give both good and bad points of living in the two locations. In the conclusion they should be clear about which they prefer and why. The children might like to support their arguments with photographs taken with a digital camera. These could be inserted into a word-processed version of the letter.

Pages 22-23 Making a living

More work on exports and imports would be a good context for learning about transport links in Scotland and geographical locations around the world. Trying to work out where the ingredients for a meal came from and plotting the possible journeys on a world map would demonstrate how Scotland relates to the rest of the world. A similar activity could be related to popular purchases by the children. How did their games machines or personal stereos get to the shops?

Writing the story of a pound, with its journey from person to person, could be used to demonstrate interdependence. This would show how everybody has a part to play in society. Alternatively, this could be done as a speaking and listening activity, with the pound passed from child to child as each adds their own bit to the pound's journey.

Pages 24-25 Getting about

This page relates closely to the development of settlements. The children could design a map. This could be completed either as a paper exercise or using ICT. Revise the use of contour lines. Draw a landscape with contour lines to show hills. Include at least one river. Swap maps with another child. Draw features onto the maps. Choose locations for settlements. Devise transport links using sensible 'rules' as to where they can go. Some examples might be:
- Trains are very poor at going up steep hills.
- Water flows downwards with the pull of gravity.
- Roads can go up steep hills but not all of the time.
- Aeroplanes need fairly large runways to land on.
This activity could also be used as a group discussion, using interactive whiteboard software which includes map symbols and the facility to draw colour-coded lines for roads etc.

Pages 26-27 Looking after the environment

These issues affect everybody. The children need to think about how they fit in with the needs of the environment. They could draw some scales and label the two sides 'good for the environment' and 'bad for the environment'. For example, if the children are prone to leaving lights on all over the house or school they should illustrate that in the 'bad' side of the scales. If they catch rainwater and use it to water the garden they should put this on the 'good' side. Write and draw things in each side of the scales. Try to think how to remedy the bad ones.

Index

Aberdeen 15, 20, 25
Aberdeen Angus 15
airports 25
Arbroath 15, 22
Aviemore 14

Balmoral 15
Ben Macdui 14
Ben Nevis 6, 14
Burns, Robert 11

Cairngorms 9, 14
Caithness glass 17
Caledonian Forest 16
call centres 23
canals 25
Central Lowlands 4, 7, 12-13, 20, 24
cities 6, 12, 13, 15, 20-1
climate 8, 9
coal 13
coasts/coastline 4, 6, 8, 10, 15, 16, 17, 20, 25
community services 22-3
continents 7
crofting 21

Dumfries 10, 11
Dundee 12, 20
Dunoon 15

Edinburgh 5, 12, 13, 20, 21, 25
electricity 23, 27
environment/environmental issues 9, 13, 14, 15, 26-7
erosion 17
exports 22, 25

Fair Isle 19
Falkirk Wheel 25
farming 10, 15, 19, 21, 23
fault lines 7
    Great Glen 7, 14, 16
    Highland Boundary 7, 12, 14
    Southern Uplands 7, 10, 12
ferries 16, 19, 25
fish farming 17, 21
fishing 10, 23
flag 5
forestry 23
forests 11, 15, 16
Fort William 15
Forth Bridges 12

Gaelic 5
gales 8, 9
Glasgow 12, 20, 24, 25
golf 13
Grampians 7, 14-15
greenhouse gases 26, 27
Greenock 25

Hebrides 18

ice ages 7, 17
industries/industrial areas 10, 12, 13, 17, 18
Inverness 15, 20, 25
islands 4, 6, 18-19, 25

Jedburgh 10
John o'Groats 16

landscape 4, 6, 7, 17, 24, 27
Leith 25

Lewis and Harris 18
lochs 6, 7, 25
    Awe 6
    Broom 17
    Katrine 13
    Lomond 13
    Linnhe 16
    Lochy 16
    Ness 16
    sea lochs 17

manufacturing 23, 26
mining 13, 25
mountains 4, 6, 7, 8, 9, 10, 14, 15, 16, 24

Nairn 15
National Scenic Areas 16, 17
North-West Highlands 7, 16-17

Oban 15
oil rigs 15, 18
Orkneys 16, 18-19

Parliament, Scottish 5, 21
population figures 5, 18, 20
ports 12, 15, 25
power stations 27
Prestwick 25

quarries 23

railways 12, 13, 14, 24
rain 8, 9, 15, 17, 27
recycling 5, 26
refuse 5, 19
rivers 6, 11, 12, 15, 21
    Clyde 12

Dee 15
Don 15
Forth 12
Spey 15
Tay 6, 12
Tweed 10
roads 10, 12, 23, 24
rocks 7

Selkirk 10
service industries 22
Shetlands 18
Skye 16-17
snow 9
Southern Uplands 7, 10-11
St Andrews 13
Stirling 20

Tain 17
temperatures 8
thistle 4
tourists/tourism 11, 13, 15, 25
towns 21
transport 12, 14, 15, 19, 24-5, 27 (see also airports, canals, ferries, railways, roads)

Ullapool 17
unitary authorities 5, 23

valleys 7, 10

waste 26
weather 8, 9
whisky 17, 23
Wick 17
winds 8, 17, 27
work, types of 22-23